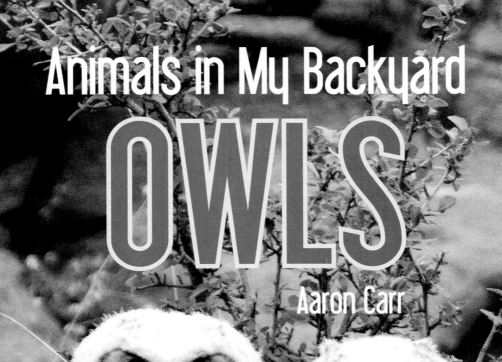

Animals in My Backyard
OWLS

Aaron Carr

LET'S READ
AV²
BY WEIGL™
ADDED VALUE • AUDIO VISUAL

Go to **www.av2books.com**, and enter this book's unique code.

BOOK CODE

A689156

AV² by Weigl brings you media enhanced books that support active learning.

AV² provides enriched content that supplements and complements this book. Weigl's AV² books strive to create inspired learning and engage young minds in a total learning experience.

Your AV² Media Enhanced books come alive with...

Audio
Listen to sections of the book read aloud.

Video
Watch informative video clips.

Embedded Weblinks
Gain additional information for research.

Try This!
Complete activities and hands-on experiments.

Key Words
Study vocabulary, and complete a matching word activity.

Quizzes
Test your knowledge.

Slide Show
View images and captions, and prepare a presentation.

... and much, much more!

Published by AV² by Weigl.
350 5th Avenue, 59th Floor New York, NY 10118
Website: www.av2books.com www.weigl.com

Library of Congress Cataloguing in Publication data available upon request.
Fax 1-866-449-3445 for the attention of the Publishing Records department.

ISBN 978-1-62127-213-7 (hardcover)
ISBN 978-1-62127-217-5 (softcover)

Printed in the United States of America in North Mankato, Minnesota
1 2 3 4 5 6 7 8 9 0 16 15 14 13 12

122012
WEP301112

Senior Editor: Aaron Carr   Art Director: Terry Paulhus

Weigl acknowledges Getty Images as the primary image supplier for this title.

Animals in My Backyard
OWLS

CONTENTS

Meet the owl.

She is a large bird with a round head.

She lives with her family when she is young.

When she is young, she stays in the nest with her family.

6

She has four sharp claws on each foot.

On each foot, she can move one claw to the front or back.

She has eyes that can not move.

With eyes that can not move, she has to turn her head to look around.

She is a bird of prey.

A bird of prey hunts other animals for food.

She flies without making noise.

Without making noise,
she sneaks up on her prey.

She stays awake at night.

At night, she looks for food to eat.

She lives in the forest.

In the forest, she can find food and water.

If you meet the owl, she may be afraid. She might fly away.

If you meet the owl, stay back.

OWL FACTS

These pages provide more detail about the interesting facts found in the book. They are intended to be used by adults as a learning support to help young readers round out their knowledge of each animal featured in the *Animals in My Backyard* series.

Pages 4–5

The owl is a bird with a round head. There are more than 200 species of owls around the world. They can range in size from 5 to 28 inches (13 to 70 centimeters) long with a wingspan between 1 and 6.6 feet (30 and 200 cm) wide. Owls can be easily recognized by their round, flat faces, rounded wings, and short tails.

Pages 6–7

Owls live in a nest with their family when young. Female owls lay between three and 11 eggs. This is called a clutch. After about 32 days, the eggs hatch. Owls time their mating season to ensure the eggs hatch when there will be plenty of food available. Young owls live in the nest until they are ready to fly on their own, usually between one and two months of age. Both parents raise their young.

Pages 8–9

Owls have four sharp claws on each foot. These curved claws, called talons, can be up to 1.4 inches (3.5 cm) long. Owls have adapted to use their talons in many ways. When hunting, owls use two talons in the front and two in the back to help them better catch their prey. When perching, however, owls often move one of their back talons to the front to get a better hold on the perch.

Pages 10–11

Owls cannot move their eyes. The owl has two large front-facing eyes. Their eyes give them excellent sight, as well as the ability to judge distances, but the eyes cannot move in their sockets like a human's eyes. Instead, the owl has to turn its head to look in other directions. The owl has a very flexible neck that can turn 270 degrees. This allows the owl to see behind itself.

Owls are birds of prey. They are part of a group of birds called raptors. Like all raptors, owls hunt other animals for food. Most owls eat small animals, reptiles, and insects. Some owls catch and eat fish, and some of the largest owls have been known to hunt animals as large as a skunk. Owls do not have teeth, so they must swallow their food whole or tear off small pieces using their hooked beaks.

Owls can fly without making noise. As a bird of prey, an owl's ability to hunt well is important for its survival. Many owl species have adapted special feathers that allow them to fly silently. An owl's primary feathers have a fringed leading edge to reduce noise and a soft trailing edge to improve stability. The wings are also covered in soft, fluffy feathers called down to further reduce noise.

Most owls are nocturnal. This means they are most active at night and sleep during the day. Owls make up half of all species of nocturnal birds. Owls use the dark of night and their ability to fly silently to better hunt their prey. These traits also help owls avoid animals that would prey on them.

Owls live in forested areas. They can be found on all continents except Antarctica. Owls thrive in many different habitats. They live in forests, grasslands, rainforests, deserts, and even parts of the Arctic. In North America, owls often inhabit wooded areas with large trees for cover and perching. They usually nest in natural hollows in the trees or in old nests left by other large birds.

If you meet the owl, keep your distance. Encountering an owl in nature is rare. Owls are solitary animals that do most of their moving around in the dark of night. However, if you do come across an owl in nature, it is best to respect the owl and maintain a safe distance. Getting too close, or making sudden movements, may scare the owl away.

KEY WORDS

Research has shown that as much as 65 percent of all written material published in English is made up of 300 words. These 300 words cannot be taught using pictures or learned by sounding them out. They must be recognized by sight. This book contains 48 common sight words to help young readers improve their reading fluency and comprehension. This book also teaches young readers several important content words. These words are paired with pictures to aid in learning and improve understanding.

Page	Sight Words First Appearance
4	the
5	a, head, is, large, she, with
6	family, her, in, lives, when, young
8	each, four, has, on
9	back, can, move, one, or, to
10	eyes, not, that
11	around, look, turn
12	of
13	animals, food, for, other
14	without
15	up
16	at, eat, night
19	and, find, water
20	away, be, if, may, might, you

Page	Content Words First Appearance
4	owl
5	bird
6	nest
8	claws, foot
9	front
12	prey
14	noise
18	forest

24